*Echoes of* Epictetus & Arrian

Cariappa Annaiah is a self-taught, eclectic artist and poet based in Greater New Orleans. Born, raised, and educated in India, he worked there for eight years in the health sciences and is now a naturalized citizen of the USA. Cariappa lived and worked in the northeast for 22 years, before re-locating to the deep south six years ago. He holds the earned designation of Copley artist at the Copley Society of Art in Boston, the oldest nonprofit art association in America. He is a member of The New England Poetry Club which was founded by Amy Lowell, Robert Frost, and Conrad Aiken in 1915. An award-winning artist, Cariappa's artwork is in private collections in the USA and abroad.

View his unique artwork at www.cariappa.net.

*(Photo credit: Self-portrait; Copyright © 2020 Cariappa Annaiah)*

Warsha Lath is a well-known and exceptional Indian artist, based in India. She trained for five years in Applied Art and graduated from the Sir J.J. School of Arts, Mumbai, one of India's best known and oldest art schools having been established in 1857. She honed her visualizing skills while working for major advertising agencies in the northeast of India, before moving to the south where she is a full-time artist. Her paintings and sketches are multi-layered, and full of Indian symbolism and meaning. Her work sells briskly and can be found in private collections in India and abroad. Be sure to view her deeply insightful and beautiful work at www.warshalathart.com.

# Echoes
# of
# Epictetus & Arrian

Cariappa Annaiah

*Illustrations* – Warsha Lath

InwardStep Publications

Cover design: Cariappa Annaiah
Cover illustration: concept, Warsha Lath and Cariappa Annaiah;
original art work, Warsha Lath; photograph of artwork Cariappa
Annaiah.

First edition
Printed in the United States of America

InwardStep Publications
Mandeville, LA
Web site: www.inwardsteppublications.com

ISBN: 978-0-9845462-2-0

Library of Congress Control Number: 2021920432

Poems were previously published as two volumes without illus-
trations:
Truisms – mostly. Reflections on life, living, and relationships.
Copyright © 2010 Cariappa Annaiah. Published in 2010 by In-
wardStep Publications.
Truisms – mostly. Reflections on life, living, and relationships.
Volume II. Copyright © 2011 Cariappa Annaiah. Published in
2011 by InwardStep Publications.
All materials in this anthology are reproduced with permission of
the author and publisher.

*Echoes of* Epictetus & Arrian

# Contents

# Cover art from Volumes I and II
*Reproduced in black and white with permission*

Truisms – mostly

Reflections on life, living, and relationships

Cariappa Annaiah

Truisms – mostly

*Volume II*

Reflections on life, living, and relationships

Cariappa Annaiah

# Dedication from Volumes I and II
*Reproduced with permission*

## Volume I

*This book is dedicated to Rani*

Dearest

Addicted
to her,
for ever.

## Volume II

*This book is dedicated to,*

*my parents, "C and A" who showed me right from wrong, and then allowed me the space to find my voice;*

*to Rani's parents, "H and H" for demonstrating by example the importance of enjoying the moment, for that is all we have in hand;*

*and, to Avaya, my maternal grandmother who lived the adage, "individuality is the spice of life."*

# Introduction

This omnibus of my published poems was 11 years in the making. In 2010 when I completed the first of two volumes, I wished to complement each poem with an illustration, akin to the work of my idol, Piet Hein. Actual visualization of an intrinsically evocative art form serves the literary equivalent of a "twofer!"

I am a good conceptualizer and visualizer, and can draw, but consider myself a line artist. Examples are the covers of volumes I and II, reproduced as black and white images in the preceding pages. Intricate drawings, fuggedaboutit!

I realized that my search for an artist who was both a great conceptualizer and illustrator would take time. The inner urge to expose my poetry trumped patience, and I published sans illustrations.

Over the ten plus years since publication of the two collections, I became aware that a compendium made sense – the 209 poems were cut from the same cloth. This time around each would be accompanied by an illustration. The search for a deeply thoughtful artist was on!

I found that artist in Warsha Lath. An excellent conceptualizer, visualizer and illustrator, a gifted painter, and a dear friend. She was right in front of me, and I missed her the first time around!

Each illustration is Warsha's interpretation of the poem. Two artists visualizing the same art form in their medium of choice. Two perspectives.

Before I address the choice of cover art and title, it is instructive to read excerpts from my introduction to the original volumes:

Truisms – mostly. Reflections on life, living, and relationships:
*These are short poems, mostly about the truisms of life and daily living. As reflected in the title of this book, not all are truisms, a few celebrate the moment or a person. I write a lot about relationships because I believe that the state of relationships, whether with spouse, kids, siblings, friends, and most definitely with oneself, determines the depth of personal happiness.*

*I am told that these poems resemble senryu, a form of Japanese poetry. Since I do not follow the rules of senryu, I think my poems are closer to the verse of American humorist Ogden Nash, and to Grooks – pithy poems penned by the Danish polymath Piet Hein.*

*The title is part of the poem. Start with the title, pause, and then read on.*

Truisms – mostly, *Volume II.* Reflections on life, living, and relationships:
*"We all have one book within us, what follows determines our status as writers," is a quote of uncertain origin that I like to attribute to R. K. Narayan, the prolific Indian author.*

*This is my second volume of short poems, mostly about the truisms of life and daily living, with special emphasis on relationships. The two volumes are independent of each other, and so need not be read in sequence; but please read both – I dare say that you will be touched in different ways.*

*The poems touch upon topics that range from the profound to the seemingly ordinary and, yes, even the risqué. They are not arranged in any order, reflecting the arbitrary appearance of truisms in real life. The ideal way to enjoy these volumes is to read a single poem at random and then stop, to reflect on the truism and its impact on your life.*

Truisms are universal and all cultures and schools of philosophy have them. In the western world, the earliest forms are found in the discourses of Greek and Roman philosophers, especially the Stoics.

Of the Stoics, Epictetus stands out. His sayings, as transcribed by his disciple Arrian, bear the closest resemblance to modern truisms. In the translations, first by Elizabeth Carter, and later by William Oldfather, there is an immediacy to the sentences and a timeless relevance to the human condition. I like to ascribe that ability to keep it real, to his humble beginnings as a slave. He had lived on both sides of the social divide and was clear-eyed.

The cover artwork traces this lineage of truisms. The rough hourglass marks the passage of time as it shows the transition from fragments of ancient Greek to modern English. And, the sides of the hourglass resemble the side profile of two faces in conversation, acknowledging the primary source of transfer of wisdom – the discourse. The torn edges on the front and back cover signify The Fragments.

The title of this anthology pays homage to the assistant. Common usage would suggest that I preface the word "assistant" with "lowly" as in lowly assistant! Why? Because, from the time of recorded history bar a few, the people who assisted "heroes" and "heroines" were written out of the historical record or, worse, not acknowledged by the beneficiaries. Of course, this category joins a long list of historically forgotten people such as – minorities of all races, religions, and sexual preferences – women – other genders.

What can I do about this injustice? Work locally, meaning, count from one and change myself, then lead by example to influence others to make change.

In this case, Epictetus in his discourses, acknowledged and echoed his teacher Rufus, and Arrian the disciple of Epictetus many years after his teacher's death decided for 'x' reasons to recollect from notes and memory, and record the discourses.

If not for Arrian the unadorned wisdom and perspective of Epictetus and Rufus would reside with the dead, across the farthest field, forever lost to humanity like so much of history.

And, you wouldn't see the title –
*Echoes of* Epictetus and Arrian.

Cariappa Annaiah

## Formatting note

Some poems are aligned to the center, others to the right or left. This is intentional **and** reflects the many ways truisms present themselves. Capitalization, punctuation, and line discipline or the absence thereof are also deliberate.

## Niceties of falsehood

The maggots
of personality.

## Trust and anxiety – the hand that rocked the box

Trust, in an old relationship
is a locked box.
Anxiety, is the hand that tugs the lock.
Test the lock once too often
and the hasp may give way
with the lock intact.

## A common malady

misconstruction.
2 plus 2 is not 22
but so often it is
just so!

## Dance is forever

laughter is too.
I wish you were here
for me and you.

You are gone
never to return
I soldier on
for me and you.

Some days I may falter
but, dance is therapy
and the young enthuse me
as they did for you.

Dance is forever
laughter is too.
Life is for living
and living I'll do
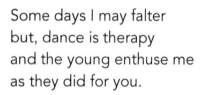 for
me and you.

This poem is dedicated to Dréa's Dream, a pediatric dance therapy program funded by The Andréa Rizzo Foundation. This national Foundation was created by Susan Rizzo Vincent to honor her only child Andréa, a graduate student in dance therapy at NYU who was killed in New York City by a drunk driver in a hit and run accident on May 19th, 2002. The poem is written from the perspective of the mother who is also a schoolteacher.

## Belief

drives humanity
in humans.
Bereft of belief
inhuman.

24 years and 364 days

or

Thoughts on the eve of our wedding anniversary

Today is yesterday in the eyes of tomorrow
Tomorrow is another day in the eyes of today.
Yesterdays add-up to milestones of yesteryears,
as we go forward and grow towards
a life of inter-twined love and understanding.

Mutual understanding,
the underpinning
of undying
ardor.

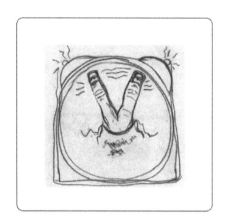

## Thoughts on a dear friend's birthday

Growing older,
you and I,
mellower and wiser – empirically.
A bulge here, and a tire there – inevitably.
Looking at Life square in the face – hopefully
and enjoying life – most definitely!

## Evolution of Lies

White lies
lie in wait
to turn black.

## Fertile as a turtle

we are.
Begetting is one thing
nurturing is something else.

People lose steam
they beget with gusto
and forget
that once you beget
you cannot forget
the nuggets of Life
you begat.

Let's review....
If you beget
Don't forget!

Sin and wash cycle

or

The color of character

Washer beware!
Too many cycles
and your character
will run.

Visit home

or

Wish it ain't so

Sitting in the garden once abloom,
watching gray clouds scud over turf-land
as the sun sets over blue-green hills
drawing the shawl of memories around you
in a vain attempt to ward off the chill
of parents in failing health.

Think before you sink,
happiness is a state of mind.
This is the cycle of Life,
you are in-cycle, why not
pedal?

## Two gifts

Wind chimes and gerberas
One tinkling
the other flourishing.
Reminders
of a comfortable friendship.

## Perils of virtue
### or
## The shakiness of pedestals

Elevate humans
and
watch them fall.
Virtue is tough
to sustain.
Snow on the ground
changes color over time.

Washing one's dirty laundry in public

Neither wash
nor
dry in public.
Private affairs
are not public
unless, you
privately
prize
public
prying
private
parts!

No presents please

Are gifts needed
for a friendship to flourish?
Of course not!
A solid relationship does not need external
accoutrements.
But, so nice to give and receive thoughtfully,
Human, that's all.

in-laws

Best
within
laws.

## Needy

Oh! So greedy.
Repeat after me,
less is more.

## The Queue

Last parent standing
is standing no more.
Loss of institutional memory
fading of a bygone era
sad.

The passing of Life past
fades in the press of the present
as you move up
The Queue.

## Lifelong friends

graying at the temples
enjoying a leisurely meal.
Feeding on sole
and
feeding the soul.

Reflections on a common odyssey

or

Why bother?

Childhood sweethearts
friends on the ship of life.

Boarded the ship of matrimony
and begat progeny
in spite of differences
in core beliefs.
Collided with the Rocks of Difference
and sank in the Bay of Indifference.
Predictably divorced,
now friends on the ship of life
once more.

Some friend – ships
are best preserved
and left at that.

Solitary and gazing at a star-studded sky
or
Two is a crowd – sometimes

Sometimes,
you find the company
of your mind
in the loneliness of a crowd.

Oftentimes,
you have to be alone
to find the priorities
of your soul.

Friendship

needs sustenance.
Make time and
stay in touch, to
stay as such.

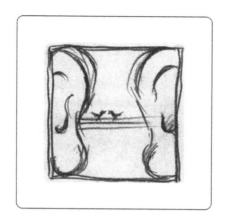

## Relationships

get musty
when
communications
get rusty.

## Self-inflicted wounds

Why in Heaven?
Don't ask Him!
Look within.

Relation ship

losing direction
in the mist
of anxiety.

## Pollution

Unfortunately, all true,
unfortunately, no clue.
Unfortunately,
unfortunate.

Ultimately, We
the People
are responsible.
Our apathy
is irresponsible.

A good relationship

is based on trust.
Not blind,
but
with eyes wide open.

## Jealousy

the fatal coronary
of a relationship.
Life is never
the same again.
*******


## Jealous lover(s)

lousy relationship(s)

## Corruption

in the body politic
is here to stay.
Woven like accidental knots
into the fabric of daily living,
by We the People.

## The appearance of disappearance

Logic
disappears
when
Lust
appears.
*******


## Wedlock – unlocked

Illicit Lust
drains
Licit Lust
and
pulverizes
Trust
into
Dust.

Trust

saunters in
when it arrives
but, sprints
when it departs.

Stay in the car! Wait for the call!

    is the mantra
    for short-term cell phone parking
    at airports.

    In the airport
    that is Life,
    we are all in
    short-term cell phone parking.
    Living Life while awaiting the call.

## Living in the Past

Don't!
The Present
needs your presence.

It's different now

or

More of the same

Lust
for power or person
in the Age of Reason,
resembles Lust
for power or person
in the Age of Unreason.

Boom!

The sound of the plane crash
hard by the airport
announced the departure
of my arriving sweetheart.

In a flash
flesh turned to ash
leaving behind
a before
and an after.

## That is the question

Ring in the new,
ring out the old!
Brave new world!
But, is the new, old,
or the old, new?

## Coin toss

Make the call
the choice is yours.
What hubris!

Fame and Fortune
Infamy and Misfortune,
coexist on both sides
of the same coin.

Anything can happen, and it will
(with apologies to Seamus Heaney)

Anything can happen
and it will.
Self-fulfilling prophecy,
a powerful tool
in the hands of the passive-aggressive.

# Wiping Shiva's Third Eye

Don't!

## The old economy

is dead.
Long live the new economy!
So say the chattering classes.
Such a waste of hot air.
There is only one economy:
the economy based on Profit and Loss.
Has always been, and
will always be.

## We the people

do as we do
for we know not, oftentimes
of a better way to do
what we do.

Human beings that we are,
we do as we do, sometimes
in spite of knowledge
that there are better ways
to do what we do.

What to do?

*******

## Call to Action

Do what you can
when you are able.

## Stereotyping

Oh! So comfortable
to stereotype.
Comfort food
for the lazy mind.
*******


## Stereotyping – redux

We all do it at times.
Stereotypes are good for laughs.
But sometimes,
stereotyping leads to consequences
of the worst kind.

## Short memories

Oppressed
de-oppressed,
Oppress!

## A Truism

Sad songs
when happy.
Happy songs
when sad.
Blues excepting.

Singing the blues to the oppressed
is like feeding lard to the well-fed.
But, the genre came from the oppressed!
Paradoxical?
Not at all!
Release,
albeit transitory –
innate.

The cancer within

Live with honor and do no evil
Tough
Live spelled backwards is evil.

Hot off the press:
innocent bystander killed in a drive-by shooting

A cold lesson
in the
randomness of existence,
delivered
by a fusillade of hot bullets.

## Work ethic

When we love
what we do.
We do –
effortlessly.

Witness for the prosecution
or
The case against open-mindedness

We see
We hear
We read
What we think.

## Headline editor

Accuse!
Torment!
Lie!
Cut-off!
Black and white words
in a gray world.
If you are looking for solutions:
acknowledge the real color
and describe the problem.
Don't give it a name.
Sensational headlines inflame an argument
not settle it.

## Self-importance
### or
## Your place on this Earth

"I take humility pills,"
said the author, Frank McCourt.*
Frankly, not easy
for the rest of the Court,
since neither we
nor our ilk
have humility skills.

*from the interview by Jesse Kornbluth for Bookreporter.com, February
19th, 1997; www.bookreporter.com/authors/au-mccourt-frank.asp.

## Art appreciation

is simple.
You like it
or you don't.
That's it.
Pshaw!
to rules and regulations.

## Old stuff – new wrinkles

So goes the adage.
Even the wrinkles are not new.
Look at the newborn
when newly born.

Better late

than The Late.
Driver,
the wheel of Life
is in your hands.

## Art and Culture

flourish when the economy is booming
wilt when indifferent, and
disappear when times are bad.
Bad economic times strip the thin veneer of civilization
to reveal the sub-human.

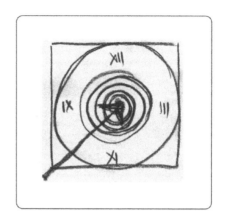

The right moment

> fleeting
> like a snowflake
> on your tongue.
> Catch it –
> swallow!

## Multitasking

is rarely productive.
Multitasking exists
because humans cannot resist.
*******


### The Multitasker

is like a drug addict.
High on a false sense of hope,
while indulging.
Low on a true sense of despair,
when done.

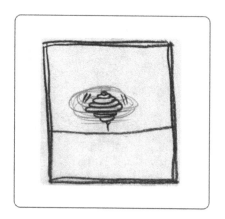

## An ode to technology

Coolly efficient
efficiently cool
when it works.

## Anticipation

I opened your e-mail eagerly
anticipating a meaningful response.
Alas,
a joke,
forwarded.

Free spirit

Constrained
Trained
More coal train, than
Coltrane.
By choice.

e-mail woes

e-mail gone AWOL
has me
climbing electronic walls!

Climbing the walls
when e-mail goes AWOL
is an exercise in electronic futility.

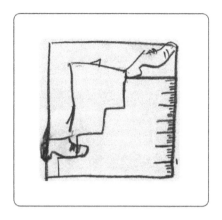

Thoughts on a well-deserved but
long overdue promotion

Given the proverbial inch,
take the proverbial mile.

Yo Men!

At home,
less of a mess
when you sit and
Go.

Thoughts on the play, Taming of the Shrew

Shakespeare
a sexist?
No,
merely a man of his times.

Racism
Sexism
Rankism,
theoretical constructs for most
unless, you're It.

## Problem solved

Problem solved.
Was there a problem?
So masculine.

## Bikini caution

Curly-Whirlies
are best kept in check,
unless you don't mind
the curly-peepers watching
every whirl!

## Christmas Stollen

you have
stolen
my heart.

Parenting riddle –
will it be a question or an affirmation?

Can you be what I want you to be?

Or

I want you to be what you can be.

Chocolate

To kill for,
too extreme.

To die for,
too drastic.

To live for,
evermore.

Yes, this panel is blank. By design. The reader is invited to draw their interpretation of the poem! Echoes the blank panel on the otherwise ornate and intricately carved Narasimha pillar in the Chennakeshava temple at Belur, Karnataka State, India,
(http://pixels-memories.blogspot.com/2015/07/sri-chennakesava-temple-complex-belur.html).
This 12th century Hindu temple complex, built by the Hoysala Dynasty, was nominated in 2014 to the Tentative List of UNESCO's World Heritage Sites and is awaiting evaluation and selection (https://whc.unesco.org/en/tentativelists/5898/).

2 in 1

parents
need
2 in 1
energy
and
2 in 1
fortitude.

Spare a thought for the teacher

when something is easy to understand.
Someone sweated a lot
to make it easy to understand.

## Three Paeans to Suzi – 1

### Suzi, the born again Recycler

Suzi the non-cycler
married Jacques the recycler
begat Payton – Drew
who knew
what to do
to get Suzi
to do as they do.
So now she
cycles and recycles
as they do.
Who knew?

## Three Paeans to Suzi – 2

### Suzi the *Paintress*

she is a Tigress.
Don't mess with her,
She will paint you over.

## Three Paeans to Suzi – 3

## Mater day paean

Wife
Mother
Shepherd
Benevolent tyrant.
The complete package,
Suzi.

## Home

idyllic country road,
songbirds on bough,
quiet sunsets –
Then.
Now,
double-yellow lines.

There is no peace
for the peaceful.

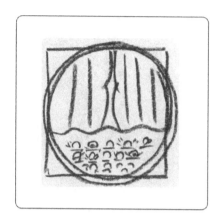

Don't bother

Why are we on this Earth?
Who knows?
Do you?

## Fighting words

"With them, without them, in spite of them,"
said cricket player Lala Amarnath.
I say,
watch them, learn from them, and win them –
over.

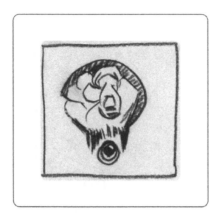

If you have to ask

why are we here
where we are.
Blame yourself
for where you are.

## Parallel Universe and other Worlds

may exist.
You are here
Exist.

## On happiness

Fax machine, fax machine,
fax me some happiness.

Fax machine, fax machine,
Fax me away
to the land
where people are happy and gay.

Can you fax machine
Can you fax me
Long messages of happiness and joy?

Aging
or
Say it ain't so

Men –
the urge to bulge
goes North!

Women –
the rack
goes
out of whack!

On memory
(with all due respect to Piet Hein)

Time
takes
things.

## Impermanence of Being

While we play
for keeps.
Keeps,
plays with us.

## Ease and Disease

One day, ease
The next, disease.
Like walking on paper
easy to tear through.

Illness

Why me?
Nothing personal,
merely stochastic.

## On loneliness

The telephone doth sit
Squat and ugly
Ring telephone, ring, ring.

## Sleep

Too little – too much,
Life dictates.
To each – their own.
*******


## Sleep – the last word

Underrated – Overrated,
Who cares?
Just sleep
and get on with it,
already.

## Whatever

Here today
Gone whenever.
So dwell less and
live more.
*******

## Whatever – revisited

Dwell less.
Not, not at all!
When it comes to thinking
less is not more.

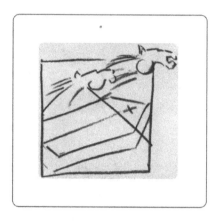

## Horses

on the racetrack called Life,
we are.

Kick sod,
sod-kicked
cross
we will
the inconstant
finish line.

Finish is certain
not the ride.

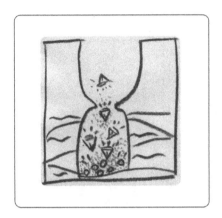

Experience –

nuggets of information
dredged from the ocean of memory
deposited on the sands of Time.

Beachcomber
your haul will vary.

## Union members

we all are!
Love it or hate it
we belong to
The Human Union.
Pick it or Picket it
the dues come due
in one form or the other.
The choice is Hobson's
not yours.

Expectations

a pregnant word
full of hope and longing
usually yields
not what you expect.

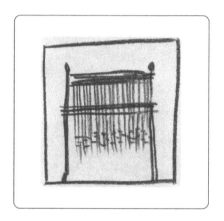

Relatedness of the unrelated

Common threads
run through
seemingly
unrelated
human actions
and
behavior.
Look for the
common thread
to understand
that the fabric of Life
is not a patchwork
of black and white
but a continuum
of swirling designs
and many colors.

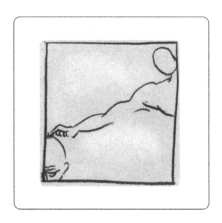

## Sense and sensibility
## (thank you Jane Austen)

Sight, smell, hearing, taste and touch
you have them
use them!

Sensing
the world
via your
senses
heightens
sensibility.

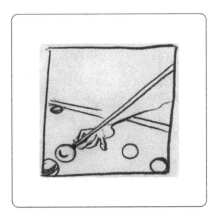

Queue in – queue out

Queue to be born.
Queue to die.
Queue not  – to live.

## Human Touch

is untouchable.

Touch
when you can
not only
when you must.

## Hospice

I hope
to never
go there.

Home is
where the
heart is.

Seldom choice
in the matter,
so there.

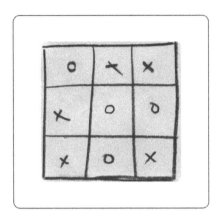

*Excel having math problems*
*Associated Press*
*3:29 PM CDT, September 28, 2007*

Excel 2007 had fleeting math problems, which inspired,

## Excel Bill

Bill's parents said,
"excel Bill."
Bill excelled,
Bill created Excel®.
Cell by cell
he became a billionaire,
but alas,
Excel cannot bill.

®Excel is a registered trademark of Microsoft Corporation.

## Memories

Chemicals,
wrapped
in the warp and weft
of Time.

Truisms

are true
as long as
humans are
beings.

I Love You

is a potent phrase.
Use responsibly.
Patent overuse
sans feeling
is a ruse.

Mistrust

the aqua regia
of
relationships.

## Hubris

Human (Hu)
beings (b)
rise (ris)
– To Fall.

## Ordinary and Extraordinary

are ordinary terms.
Just be
the best
that you
can be.
And,
stay in one piece
by being at peace
with what you
can be.

## Winner

be aware.
For every winner
there are a host
of almost winners
who but for you
go they.

## The Ties that bind

our past, present and future
are strands of The Common Thread
that runs through our lives.

Constant chatter

without
matter
makes
us no
better
than the
Mad Hatter.

Insight

is better than
no sight
but
does not mean
that the end
is in sight.
*******


Insight

is the first step
in the problem-solving staircase
not
the only step!

## The unbalance of imbalance

Beauty
external
unmatched
by beauty
internal
is beautiful
to behold
but not to
hold.

The imbalance of Beauty
unbalances
the best of
beautiful
beauties.

## Helping the Helper

Look after yourself
while
looking after others,
else
others will have to
look after you.

## Relationship

based on Beauty and Lust
will not last
since Beauty and Lust
will not last.

## Reinforce

is the word of the day
today, and every day.

Reinforce in equal measure
patience and equanimity –
the forces that rein in
the forces that rain on your parade.

Muse: a conversation with medical and graduate student IAN.

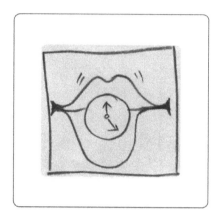

## Silence is golden

most of the time,
but at times
gold can turn to lead
when silence at the wrong moment
could lead one away
from the
mother lode.

Timing is not everything.
Timing is the only thing!

## Selfish help

Selfless
is helpless
if self-help
is less.

Contemplate

calmly
by
canceling
cacophony.

## Descartes rephrased
## (with a nod to Buddha and Bob*)

I breathe, therefore I am
alive.
I am alive, therefore I can
think.
Mistake not,
breathing
for
thinking.

*Robert Rowland Smith, author of the wonderfully thoughtful book, "Breakfast with Socrates: An extraordinary (philosophical) journey through your ordinary day," published by Free Press in 2010. The author's introduction was my muse for this poem.

## Lost and not found

"Yourself lost"
is not a state
in which to
look for The Lost.

Success without the excess

Success is a heady thing.
The head rarely can handle
the excess that success brings.

To prove the adage that
success begets success,
beat down the hubris
that success brings,
suck the excess
out of success,
and focus
on what brought on success.

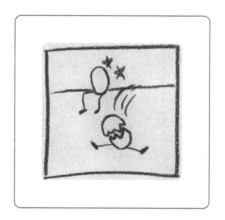

## Success with the excess

The nexus between
success and excess
has a knack
of kicking you
in the solar plexus.

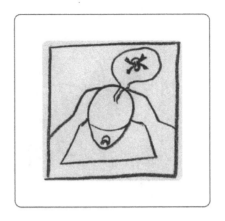

False prophets of doom

et tu?
me too!

## Mother's day – Father's day

Remember your parents
on one Day
if you must.

But remember,
your parents
remember you
everyday.

Equality

a rarity
for the majority
of society.

## All Points Bulletin
### or
## Thomas Carlyle nailed it

Be wary,
an animal clothed
is similar to
an animal unclothed.

Covering the private bits
of animals and humans
does not make
an animal a bit more human
or,
a human a bit less of an animal.

## Solvation

Inaction
is action
if
inaction
is the best solution.

Procrastination

Inaction
with the promise of
action.

Give chance a chance

Once and done
is better than
not once, and done.

When you chance your Life

in the fast lane to Death
may friends
appear in your rear-view mirror,
lights flashing – horns blaring,
and pull you over
to give a tongue-lashing
and, a summons
for a second chance.

Take heed.
Life,
rarely gets a
second chance.

A Massachusetts State Police officer was the spark for this poem;
he did not give me a tongue-lashing but did hand me a speeding
ticket – my first, and hopefully, my last.

Life goes on – really
or
Calling all indispensables

Independent
able, and
responsible
but,
indisputably
dispensable.

Salve or salvation?

Mail box gone.
Lights are on.
Deterrent?
Hardly!
Merely salve
for the quaking soul.

A stolen mail box was the muse for this poem.

Problems you choose to ignore

will
– not go away
– come your way
– come in your way
and,
will not go away.

## Age in Marriage

Married for the ages?
or,
Marred for the ages?
or,
Married until the other ages?

## Goodness

only in the limelight
is less
than good.

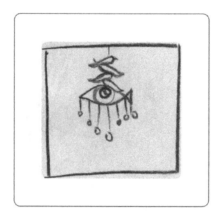

Hark!

Beware of the cess in success.
Don't "bad cess to"* success
by living a life of excess.

*bad cess to, Irish phrase: a curse on.

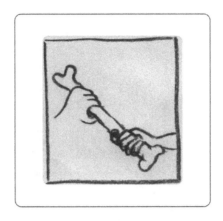

## Universal Truth

No unity
when there is
opportunity.

Marriage

a work in progress
till death do us apart.

## Mary and Ed – the sad story

Married in a hurry
tried to be merry
ended up sorry.

Mary met Harry.
Ed strayed with Ted.
That was the end of Mary and Ed.

A lucid moment of introspection
or
Plumbing the depths of human nature

reveals
a price to sellout
and,
a prize to seek out.

## Don't quake only when the Earth shakes

The earth shakes
and we humans quake.
We lie awake
as the earth wakes.

Let us hope in the future
our conscience quakes
and our bodies shake
before we undertake
to take the untaken.

## The Untaken

don't want to be taken.
Be sure you have
what it takes
to takedown
The Untaken.

## Question to the married

You married when firm.
Will you stay together
when the other is infirm?

Elevate at your own risk

Sex is a physiological response
no more.
Elevating sex to anything else
will surely make you
an "ex."

Cede not

lucidity.

Married –

are you harried
and hurried?
Pause, and take stock
else, you may not stay married.

## Child less in childhood

Children
having
children
ruin
childhood
for
children.

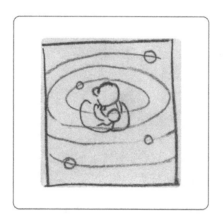

The day before and after

Mother's day
is
mother's day.

Parents cannot be relegated
to a "day,"
they are here to stay.

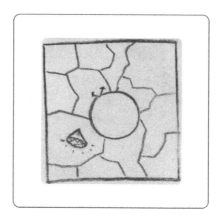

In marriage we trust, until

opportunity knocks.
Hunter and the quarry
have a quandary.
Pebbles on the glass, or
a rock through the marital window?

Space and Time
or
Archaic words one too many, but
archaic thoughts none too many

Before your relationship
is torn asunder
and your eyes wander
go yonder
and ponder
why your relationship
is being torn asunder.

## Whiff is not enough

Mere spoor
of the spouse
is of no use
around the house.

Human

behavior
often
needs a savior.

## Janus in Us

Lust sans love
and
love sans lust
can co-exist.

Resist,
if you want your
relationship to exist.

Opportunity

limits
fidelity.

Absence

may make the heart
go fonder
but,
the lawn
grows longer!

"L" words both, that's all

Lusting after lust
is often mistaken
for
lusting after love.

## Achievement is rarely a fluke

Tenacity and persistence
key attributes of
Nature's existence.

Those attributes
with
no attitude
are required
to achieve
anything of
magnitude.

## Black and white, not black or white

Night becomes day
and day becomes night
in gradual shades
of black and white.

We Humans wish
that we could stop
the time of flight,
and call something
black or white.

Learn from the day
learn from the night
that there is no true
black or white.

No ulterior motive
or
Keep it simple

I care
so,
I share.

## No quarter given, and sadly, none expected

Humans
treating
humans
inhumanly
cannot call themselves
humans,
and expect
humanity
to treat them as
humans.

## Cultures

through the ages
have clashed
and slashed,
over the premise
"I am right, and you are wrong."

People of Culture,
please
be cultured
and consider
"I am right, and you are not wrong"
before you use your might
to "right" the "wrong."

## Question for the ages

How do you
get from here to there
when all you have is
here and now?

Find a mentor,
not a tormentor
who is here,
and was there.

Befriend the aged,
they have been there.
Free them from the
cage of age
as they free you from
the ague of vague.

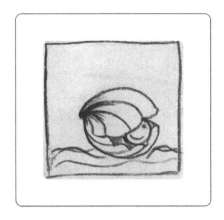

Friend

till The End
is The Friend
to find.

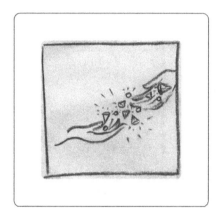

Advice

is wise
as long as it does not
advise vice
or,
hold you in its vise.

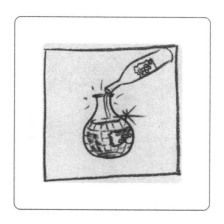

Generational hot air
or
Isn't it funny that

the rocky bottom recedes,
as the younger generation
slides down in esteem
of the older, even as
the older generation
grudgingly cedes to the younger,
all the while regurgitating
on their successors
the negative feelings
of their predecessors?

# The friendship

of friends
who are friends
only when it is
convenient to be friends
is a friendship of convenience

## Just deserts

Treat people like they are disposable
and, you will be disposed of
when they are able.

## Think before you spout off

People are receptive
to the confident emission
of a measured response.
Neither uncontrolled
nor premature.

The liquid theme of this poem was inspired by MZ, a hydrologist.

## Oasis in our life

we all need one
lucky ones have one.

To shelter in the shade of non-judgmental
friends,
who will douse you with the cold water of
reality, and
have you partake in the communal meal of
congeniality.

Providing a perspective
that cannot be obtained
by being introspective.

Pick on someone your size

Don't go to war
in the boudoir.

## Hard fact of Life

Nature
does not nurture
creatures.
Creatures
nurture
their own
and,
prey on other
creatures.

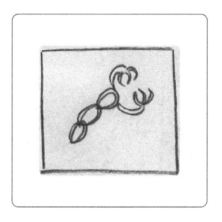

## In Humans We Trust

We humans
tinker with The Code
because we can decode.

As we humans
tinker with The Code
because we can,
please let us tinker
to conquer
the canker
of inhumanity.

Isn't it a pity

that inhumanity
resides in humanity?

Men

be manly
with the family.

A Public Service Announcement against domestic violence.

## Make your choice

Live forever
Live in ferment
Live in fear, or
Live every fleeting moment.

Lip service

is best
not served.

## Lest we forget

Count your blessings
now and then,
as you count
your money,
every penny!

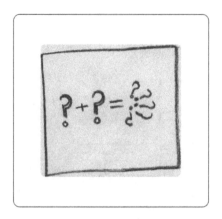

Calling all policy-makers, ideologues,
arm-chair specialists, bloggers, and lay-
persons
(That includes Me, You, and Ours.)

Problems beset the world,
as we are beset by problems.

Spare us this day
yet another way
of rendering
the far too rendered.

Give us this day
a realistic way
to solve the problems, and
resolve the differences.

Imperfection in perfection

Imperfection
is so Human, and
perfection
so Divine.

Humans
are of many hues, but
Divine we are not.

Seek divinity by all means,
but have the humility to know
that you are not the Divinity.

Empathy

is not easy
when you are
empty of pity.

## Impossible alliance

Imperfect humans
seeking perfection
in an imperfect world.

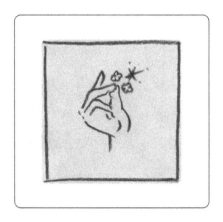

## Easy

to be queasy
of the human condition.

Before accepting queasy
as the new easy,
ask yourself,
do you easily become queasy?

If queasy is the new easy,
ease the queasiness and,
quell the uneasiness
by answering the answerable –
which part of the queasiness
can I make less queasy?

Speak-up!

Don't depend on telepathy
to show empathy.

## Strive for your dreams

Take what you can get
but, don't be taken by
what you get,
or worse,
be taken for a ride
by those
who have got you.

## Educators dilemma
### or
## Art of diplomacy

Leave me alone, if I
Don't want to.
Teach me, if I
Don't know how.
Persuade me, if I
Don't want to know how.

Greed

is more
when more
is less.

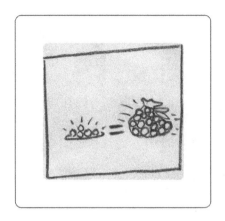

Stress

is less
when less
is more.

## Freedom

unrestricted, and free
taken for granted,
like the air we breathe in.
Brethren, we hardly notice it
until we lose it.

## Tribalism

a schism-inducing
ism.

Obsession

over possession
leads a relationship
to Perdition.

Humans take note!

Freedom
can become serfdom,
if it is not acknowledged
freely in the kingdom.

Love

someone.
Possess no one.
Obsess over none.

Let not the halo blind you
or
Easy to be

– philanthropic when you are rich

– loving, when your love is blooming

– magnanimous when you have no animus

– kind to your own kind.

– easy, when the going is easy.

Fool!

Don't look for a menu
to order
ardor.

## If

you are poor
work more.
And, hopefully
one day
you will be poor
no more.
 *******

## If

you are rich
don't bitch
about your itch.
Have you seen the people
who do not have even a stitch?

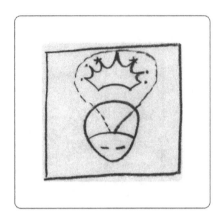

# Delusion*

is an illusion
that in profusion
can lead to confusion.

*The muse for this poem was the novel "Don Juan de Marco,"
by Jean Blake White based on the screenplay by Jeremy Le-
ven, and published in 1995 by Signet, an imprint of Dutton
Signet, a division of Penguin Books USA Inc. This beautifully
written and lyrical novel is a multi-layered, and non-judgmental
exploration of two states of mind – the delusional, and the pre-
retirement. It is a worthy read for anyone interested in either
topic. Jean Blake White is a gifted, and talented writer, poet,
and artist. The screenplay was made into a movie of the same
name by New Line Cinema, starring Marlon Brando, Johnny
Depp, and Faye Dunaway, and directed by Jeremy Leven.

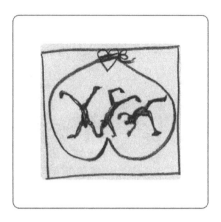

Much ado and no ardor

You are unlikely
to be stiff in the back and,
the "bone,"
if all you can do
is talk up a storm.

## PMAD*

People making a difference
in this world of indifference
make the difference
by overcoming their own indifference.

*PMAD is the in-house abbreviation used by staff at the Christian Science Monitor to refer to, "People making a difference" the last page feature managed by Greg Lamb which runs in every issue of the weekly. The acronym was mentioned in "Upfront" the weekly column by Monitor editor John Yemma (TCSM, volume 102/issue 44, page 5, September 27, 2010).

Beholder, don't eye!
or
Nudity

is crude
decries
the prude.

How rude! cries the nude,
to equate nudity with crudity.
Nudity is about solidarity
with your nativity, and
not about the itty-bitty.

Nudes, be subdued
around prudes.
Prudes, consider it rude
to stare at nudes.

## The Spectrum

is not merely
in the color of our skin,
since we sink into place
on the bell-shaped curve
of human behavior.

So remember,
when it comes to behavior,
you are neither
superior nor inferior;
you differ only to a degree
from the duffer.

Let it hang out
or
Ode to the Artist

To create unique art
tryst not
with preconceived notions,
lest the conceptus be tainted
by the conceit of notions.

## Hope

like love can come in a rush
but is easily crushed.
Don't purport to offer hope
if you cannot proffer support.

Normality

is an oddity
in the normal distribution
of human behavior.

## Reality

is comfortable
with complexity.

We humans
crave simplicity
but create
complexity.

Humanity,
to maintain sanity
understand, and accept
the complexity of reality.

The seduction

of perfection
is a distraction
from attraction.

## Problems

have a propensity
of propagating
false intensity and,
coalescing into a
towering thundercloud
that promotes
cowering anxiety, and
hide in the basement –
inactivity.

Akin to Thor of yore
use a hammer, this one
forged in practicality,
to break-up the cloud of unreality,
into itty-bitty
addressable
reality.

Integrity

integral
to
greatness.

## Towering waste of mental capacity

Towering theoretician
combined with
towering impracticality
yields a
towering
tiresome
twit.

Recognize the recognizable

Gild not
guilt.

Life

is the hash
that happens,
when there is
a long dash
between
intent
and
action.

Cheating

at eating
shows
in the fitting!

Emotional closure

is closer
once you regain
composure.

## End game

Can do
will do
going to do
and doing,
are not synonyms for
Done!

# Acknowledgments

I thank Jennifer Dubin for editing this collection. Jen is an uncommon editor, since her literary skill set is matched with a wide and deep experience herding cats! Those attributes came in handy, interacting with a poet irreverent to poetry orthodoxy! Did I mention that she is a good human?

I acknowledge that all living humans make mistakes, and at last check I have a pulse. I am responsible for all errors that crept into the book spanning ideation to publication.

The title of this compendium acknowledges the assistant and broadly those who helped. Reflecting that spirit, acknowledgements from Volumes I and II are reproduced verbatim:

Volume I: *I wish to thank Daphne Bell for her role as de facto editor. However, I take responsibility for typos, and errors of omission or commission. To my friends who functioned both as a gauntlet of critics as well as my cheering squad: Daphne Bell, Suzi Lazo, Jovita Crasta, Bobby Cherayil, Nandini Sengupta, Warsha Lath, Goutam Lath, Marie Selsky, Larry Selsky, Kendra Taylor, Michelle Connole, Catharine Chase, Ramnik Xavier, Marc Zimmerman, Mary Jacob, Dorothy (Dottie) Binford, Ravi Bhavnani, Steve Pirnie and Tetsu Hayashida – thank you very much. Shoba Srinatha, my sister, thank you for checking to make sure that the poems did not reflect the state of my mind at the time of writing – no, they didn't! Finally, thanks too, to my wife, Amitinder Kaur who is also my primary critic and filter.*

Volume II: *I wish to thank Daphne Bell for her reprise role as de facto editor. However, as before, I take responsibility for typos, and errors of omission or commission. To my vetting group who continue to give me prompt, and precise feedback: Daphne Bell, Suzi Lazo, Jovita Crasta, Bobby Cherayil, Warsha Lath, Kendra Taylor, Ramnik Xavier, Dorothy (Dottie) Binford – thank you very much. My sisters, Revathy Belliappa, Shoba Srinatha, and Indira Ganapathy, and Rani's brother, Gurkamal Chatta, and sister, Deepa Bhushan – thank you for the support, and feedback. Finally, thanks too, to my wife, Amitinder Kaur for her sentinel role as my primary critic and grounded filter.*

# Notes

Warsha Lath's illustrations are loaded with meaning and symbolism, just like her paintings. As an aid to the reader, here are her notes for each panel in order of appearance. The writing is lightly edited for clarity, and retains her voice, tone, and syntax. *Numerals denote page numbers. Italics are my comments.*

1   All is an act. An act of changing faces and colors.
2   Two hands joined in trust form the key to happiness in a relationship.
3   Because all of life is an illusion.
4   Dance is self-expression: a free spirit.
5   Light a beacon of light and hope at the end of a tunnel of despair.
6   Celebrations of togetherness and true love.
7   The clock of our lives ticks on; happy in each other's company and in each moment.
8   In Indian mythology, a black crow pecks liars; like white mushrooms that molt and turn black.
9   Prosper and thrive but don't forget your roots.
10   Like watercolors run. The coiling snake depicts sins.
11   The whirlpools called Life. Paper boats are us. Boats floating in the whirlpools of Life and sinking with time – natural.
12   Like two peanuts packed comfortably and naturally inside the pod. No pushing each other for space.
13   Tainted heroes set on pedestals fall like a broken star.
14   Lock them with the key which is with you and for you only.
15   Gift your friends your heart full of sincerity and warmth.
16   Let them live within the Line Of Control!
17   Don't be like a pig.

18  Parents are solid pillars of strength, but they have to fall. Such is Nature's way.
19  Two souls, one heart, feeling each other's feelings – that's lifelong friendship.
20  Some relationships, however old should remain as they began.
21  Like a seagull, alone, but never lonely, flying high.
22  Keep the sweet communication ongoing with your friends. Find time with flowers and cards.
23  When you stop hearing from each other.
24  Like digging your own grave.
25  A paper boat – relationship lost in a sea of anxiety; the lighthouse – a good relationship which guides the lost boat.
26  The drooping and dying flowers symbolize humans who will die and wither due to the self-created problem of pollution.
27  A good relationship and its anchor – trust which is transparent.
28  Relationship – a fragile and beautiful glass vase. The flowers – love and happiness which droop and die when jealousy intervenes. Like a broken vase, a relationship once broken, can never be fixed perfectly again.
29  Root cause of all corruption – I – Ego. Keep it small, then see…
30  Like a knife tearing you apart. Like a snake filling you with distrust.
31  Like a comet, can appear and disappear in a blink.
32  We await our name to be called at the finish line.
33  Memories good or bad. Like film negatives of the past, the mind flies back in the oceans of time.
34  The crown and the King's throne symbolizing power overpowering reason.

35 Remembrances and grief, like dried leaves floating in the wind, in the book of memories finding dried flowers given by a loved one.

36 The pendulum of time, swinging back and forth.

37 Like tossing the coin or finding your fortune with tarot cards.

38 Lightning can strike anywhere, anytime.

39 It's the Third Eye!

40 Like basic arithmetic which is a constant through the ages.

41 Don't have flock mentality.

42 On and on, like an unstoppable gramophone record.

43 The donkey is a symbol of oppression.

44 Like having a pearl in your grasp for a short time — transient enjoyment. *Crows, one of the most intelligent of the animal kingdom are known to leave gifts for those who feed them — a phenomenon called gifting.*

45 Like a spider spinning its barely visible web to trap prey.

46 A paper boat caught in whirlpools.

47 A happy mind blossoming.

48 Mind follows its own compass.

49 The power of writing.

50 A bloated 'me.'

51 You either like it or don't. Art is in the eye of the beholder.

52 Like an old shoe with creases and cracks and gift-wrapped. Like old wine in a new bottle.

53 Haste is fatal.

54 Make hay while the sun shines.

55 Hit the bull's eye at the right moment.

56 Like a juggler, miss one ball and everything goes topsy-turvy.

57 Like a spinning top moving smoothly on a tightrope.

58 Every rose has thorns. Expectations can hurt!

59 Set oneself free with imaginary wings.

60 Lay the wreath in despair.

61 Try and leap a few steps to ascend faster.

62 Clean and neat, happy home.

63 Humans like chess pieces, are equal when jumbled in the box.

64 Like a fly on the nose, just swat it away!

65 Beware!

66 Symbolized heart, symbolizing love.

67 A duckling who wants to fly rather than do what is expected of it — to swim obediently.

68 Intentionally blank.

69 Superwoman and superman, or super-them holding their little star and flying.

70 A halo for the dedicated teacher.

71 Just like a puppet on 'their' strings.

72 Fierce, don't cross her path!

73 Queen bee and busy bee.

74 Once peaceful, now just a picture in memory.

75 Just actors doing our parts on the stage of Life.

76 Power in the pen.

77 Any use pointing a finger at others?

78 Just a speck in the vast Universe, but at least that. Be joyous.

79 Messages from everywhere to make me smile.

80 Ballooning with time.

81 Time is a stealthy robber, every minute snatched. It will wait for none.

82 What you sow, so shall you reap.

83 Life is a balancing tightrope walk.

84 Happens to everybody, everywhere. Stop self-pity.

85 No man is an island.

86 Oh, for the 'honey-heavy dew of slumber' – Shakespeare's Julius Caesar.

87 Let the mind be always positively ignited.

88 We shall all cross the line (of Life).

89 The hourglass of Time.

90 Like a busy, bee union in a beehive.

91 Like the parched Earth waiting for rain clouds that only fly away.

92 Like the warp and weft of fabric. Interwoven.

93 Touch and feel.

94 Like billiard balls, one after another, waiting to go.

95 Reach out at every opportunity.

96 To recover happily at home with homely care.

97 Noughts and crosses that don't match.

98 Intricate designs of a million remembrances in beautiful designs.

99 The seed of truth that germinates with truly beautiful thoughts.

100 Be careful how you use these three words, 'I love you' like lighting a fire and or setting-off an explosion.

101 It's poison that will kill a beautiful bond.

102 Because, even the Sun has to set.

103 Believe and be confident of yourself.

104 It's touch and go. Every success wears a crown of thorns.

105 The three strands, past, present, and future weave the beautiful tapestry of Life.

106 Or, like parrots!

107 Like a ladder that you climb, slowly and steadily, step by step to the light.

108 Like a giddy-headed butterfly.

109 After all, doctors are also humans.

110 An integrated relationship of two hearts and minds will last forever.

111 Be peaceful to reinforce.

112 To speak at the right moment and right time.

113 Self-help is best.

114 Deliberate peacefully.

115 Alive with deep thinking.

116 Find yourself by yourself.

117 Success is like getting drunk and losing one's head; maintain self-control to keep your feet on the ground.

118  Pride and excess come before a great fall.
119  Don't get carried away by others.
120  Parents love for you with all their heart is 365 days.
121  Very few believe this.
122  Some of us **are** like beasts within.
123  Learn patience.
124  Hibernating till a better tomorrow.
125  Like roulette, try it once. Take a chance.
126  Speed thrills, but can kill.
127  All of us, ultimately dispensable, unto mud we will go.
128  Take precautions, nevertheless anything can happen anytime. *Illustration shows the iconic, British, red, pillar post box, common in Commonwealth countries including India.*
129  Like a dagger, always on your head.
130  Too many question marks ???????? in this Institution.
131  Theatrical goodness is no good.
132  Ward off the evil eye for good luck only.
133  Grab and think only of yourself.
134  Behind a home of happy hearts, sunshine day after day.
135  A House of Cards.
136  Temptation like the forbidden apple, everyone falls prey.
137  Our conscience is our alarm, listen, wake up and take heed.
138  Like the type of Mahatma Gandhi.
139  To walk together through rain and sun, illness and happiness, true love is the strongest shelter.
140  Trashed, if just a lusty beast.
141  Be clear, like a transparent glass of clear water.
142  Quality time and communication, find time for these in your marriage.
143  Like puppets, their hands bound in the unhappiness of premature responsibilities.

144  Parents like the Sun, a constant in our lives.

145  And the rock from the trust-band falls.

146  Before the mast is torn to shreds in your stormy relation ship.

147  No point in being a constantly transparent companion.

148  We pray for angels around us.

149  Just lust is a big NO for a happy and loving relationship.

150  Don't be a bee, dancing from one flower to another.

151  All work on the backburner as the heart pines.

152  Wolf love is no love, just lust.

153  Those two keys play together to achieve beautiful results.

154  Life is the shade card of tonal grays with no distinct black or white. Like a crow, seemingly black but actually deep shades of grey.

155  Share with just love.

156  Humans keep humans in bondage.

157  Instead of always pointing fingers, try to understand why the other is pointing a finger.

158  Benefit from their friendship, their experience and wisdom.

159  A true friend is like a rare pearl, difficult to find.

160  Just passion the gems of wisdom.

161  Just like old wine in new bottles.

162  Fair weather friends are not true friends.

163  Respect others, else you will join them in the bin you created for them.

164  Please let out steam only when required and at the correct time.

165  Good, true friends are like sheltering trees.

166  Please battle with your physical equal.

167  Like poisonous mushrooms.

168  The DNA with claws.

169  Behind the beatific face of Humanity.

170  Be a Lion of your den.

171 Be courageous and fly high over the Ocean of Life, like a seagull.
172 Understand deeply and follow.
173 Save and count your blessings for a rainy day.
174 Problems + Problems resulting in a multitude of problems.
175 Instead of a BIG I (full of ego), keep a small 'I' and feel divine (in goodness and humility).
176 Please don't be stone-hearted so that others have to use a pick.
177 Or just dreaming of castles in the air.
178 Snap your fingers and decide to get rid of your queasiness.
179 Communicate clearly. Don't leave it to telepathy.
180 Reaching for your dreams can result in being taken for a ride.
181 Educating is an art.
182 More…I need more!
183 Contented with what you have.
184 Never underestimate the value of Freedom.
185 Sheep mentality.
186 Love darts constantly pricking the brain.
187 Prisoners in the name of Freedom.
188 Set love free.
189 Like crocodile tears, the ulterior motive is not easy to spot. *Crocs and alligators shed tears not because they are feeling remorse but to lubricate their nictitating membrane while on land.*
190 Search in your own heart for your menu of ardor.
191 Two sides of a coin, on one side the poor ant is toiling and hoping. On the other is the proud peacock looking askance at the others.
192 Living in a fantastic and unreal world.
193 No use in 'blah, blah' or doing cartwheels to prove yourself.

194 They are the stars, the brave angels.
195 The human body is a piece of art, nothing crude.
196 Everyone is equal like the different colors which make the rainbow.
197 Set your canvas aflame in your mind and ideas.
198 Like the gust of wind, don't crush the vase of love and hope.
199 They stand apart.
200 It's like a complex puzzle which we strive to solve.
201 Not everyone can be Mona Lisa.
202 They strike through the clouds of anxiety like bolts of lightning.
203 It is standing tall amongst the others.
204 Towering nothing.
205 Zoom in close to recognize better.
206 Then it becomes a jump too far.
207 Mind the inches that slowly grow, but will never seem to go.
208 Be Buddha-like.
209 Check-mate – The End.

# Subject Index

# Title Index

CPSIA information can be obtained
at www.ICGtesting.com
Printed in the USA
LVHW080444181121
703571LV00015B/835